ETHEREAL GUARDIANS

A radiant presence, cloaked in light, stands eternal, guarding with silent grace and unwavering devotion.

WINNIE VANDANA MEHRA

INDIA • SINGAPORE • MALAYSIA

Hardcase 979-8-89588-351-8
Paperback 979-8-89556-379-3

With gratitude to God for his guidance ,to my parents for their unwavering love and to my husband for his endless support

Authors Note

If you're holding this book, it's not just because you're curious about angels—it's because the angels themselves are calling you to discover their presence. As you delve into these pages, you'll begin to witness their work in your life in ways that are impossible to ignore.

Understanding angels is crucial, for humanity is constantly influenced by the voice of angels or fallen angels. The path you choose depends on the guidance you seek.

Once you embrace the reality of angels, God will command His angels to protect you in all your ways. It's vital to recognize the power and significance of angels.

Angels are not to be worshipped or placed above God, for they too are created beings.

This book aims to open your eyes to the unseen yet powerful realm that surrounds us. Just as the wind can be felt but not seen, the presence of angels is meant to be experienced, not worshipped. Through these pages, you'll learn to recognize and understand their influence, feeling their presence as they work in your life. This book will guide you in acknowledging their existence and role, bringing the invisible world to light.

Index

Preface

In these pages lies the wisdom of the eternal, a guide for the soul's journey through life's deepest questions. Each word is a spark, kindling the light of truth and love within. Let this divine message inspire, comfort, and awaken your spirit as you walk the sacred path of understanding. Open your heart, and let the voice of the divine echo through your soul.

01

Who Are Angels?

Across various religions, the belief in angels as supernatural beings is widespread. The theological study of angels is called "Angelology."

Angels are created beings, made by God before humans. Unlike us, they are made of fire and spirit. Though often portrayed as winged beings, angels are actually spirits without a fixed form. Just like water can exist as ice, liquid, or vapor depending on its environment, angels can change form when needed. While they may appear in different shapes to fulfil their roles, they are ever-present on Earth, working in different areas as assigned by God.

In Abrahamic religions, angels are seen as benevolent messengers, acting as intermediaries between God and humanity, helping to guide and protect.

The Difference Between Angels and Humans

1. Angels were created before humans

God first created angels, then humans.

2. Angels live forever

Unlike humans, angels don't experience death. When humanity sinned, death entered the human experience, but our spirits, made in the image of God, are eternal. This is why there is an ongoing spiritual battle. Fallen angels want humans to face the same fate as them. But as John 3:16 tells us, "Christ came to save us so that whoever believes in Him shall not perish, but have eternal life."

3. Angels are ministering spirits

According to Hebrews 1:14: "Are not all angels ministering spirits sent to serve those who will inherit salvation?" Angels carry out miracles and minister to those who have inherited salvation. However, they only respond to the instructions of those who are saved.

4. Angels Follow Commands

Angels are pure and holy beings, created by God to serve Him. They stand in His presence, carrying out His will without question. Unlike humans, angels don't have free will; they act in complete obedience to God. We've all heard the story of Satan (formerly Lucifer), a powerful archangel who rebelled against God. His pride led him to try to make himself equal to God, but just like it's unthinkable for a creation to rival its creator, Satan's rebellion was utterly intolerable in heaven. As a result, he and the angels who followed him were cast out.

These fallen angels, now working against God's will, tempt humans to stray from the path God laid out for us. Satan's fall is recorded in Isaiah 14:12-14:

"How you have fallen from heaven,

You star of the morning, son of the dawn!

You have been cut down to the earth,

You who defeated the nations!

But you said in your heart,

'I will ascend to heaven; I will raise my throne above the stars of God,

And I will sit on the mount of assembly,

In the recesses of the north.

I will ascend above the heights of the clouds;

I will make myself like the Most High.'"

And in Revelation 12:9, the Bible describes how Satan and his angels were expelled from heaven:

"The great dragon was hurled down—that ancient serpent called the devil, or Satan, who leads the whole world astray. He was hurled to the earth, and his angels with him."

After being thrown to Earth, Satan tempted Eve in the Garden of Eden, convincing her to disobey God's one command: not to eat from the tree of the knowledge of good and evil. You might wonder, what's the big deal about eating a piece of fruit? Think of it like this: if you told your child not to watch TV and to focus on their homework while you're out, but when you return, you find them watching TV, won't you be upset about what they're doing—it's the disobedience that hurts. In the same way, Adam and Eve's disobedience grieved God, leading to their banishment from the Garden of Eden. Afterward, God placed cherubim to guard the entrance to the garden, as described in Genesis 3:24:

"After He drove the man out, He placed cherubim and a flaming sword flashing back and forth to guard the way to the tree of life."

5. Angels Carry God's Messages

Angels often appear in human form or visit people in dreams to deliver messages from God. For example, in Genesis 18, God sent an angel to tell Abraham that his wife, Sarah, would conceive and bear a son, Isaac.

Similarly, in Matthew 1:18-25, an angel appeared to Joseph in a dream, telling him that Mary's child was conceived by the Holy Spirit and that he should take her as his wife. The angel told Mary to name the child Jesus, as He would save His people from their sins.

Do Angels Have Emotions?

Yes, angels experience emotions, but they are expressed in a holy way. They feel joy, sorrow, and even anger, all in line with God's will. Angels don't hold grudges or impose their own desires; they follow God's instructions and respond to the prayers of believers.

They Rejoice When Sinners Repent

In Luke 15:10, Jesus said, "There is joy in the presence of the angels of God over one sinner who repents."

Angels celebrate every time a person turns back to God.

They Continually Praise God

Angels are constantly praising God and expect humanity to do the same. As it says in Psalm 148:2:

"Praise Him, all His angels; Praise Him, all His hosts!"

And in Isaiah 6:3, angels proclaim, "Holy, Holy, Holy is the Lord of hosts; the whole earth is full of His glory!"

Angels Get Angry Too

Angels, especially Archangel Michael, are described as righteous warriors who lead God's armies against evil forces. In Revelation 12:7-12, Michael leads the angels in battle against Satan and his demons. His anger is a righteous, holy anger that compels him to fight for the good of humanity and for God's will to prevail.

Angels are powerful spiritual beings who carry out God's commands, protect and guide us, and feel deeply for the fate of humanity. They're not distant like otherworldly creatures—they are actively involved in our lives, rejoicing, protecting, and fighting for us in ways we often can't even see.

Angels Get Angry

In Numbers 22, we see a clear example of an angel expressing anger when witnessing wrongdoing. When Balaam, a man on a misguided mission, abuses his donkey, the angel of the Lord intervenes with a stern rebuke.

In Numbers 22:32-33, the angel says, "Why have you beaten your donkey these three times? I have come here to oppose you because your path is a reckless one before me. The donkey saw me and turned away from me these three times. If it had not turned away, I would certainly have killed you by now, but I would have spared it."

This shows that angels, though holy, can express righteous anger when they see humans acting in ways that contradict God's will.

Angels Get Sorrowful

Angels also feel sorrow when humans fail to live up to God's expectations. A striking example occurs in Luke 1:8-20, when the angel Gabriel visits Zechariah in the temple. Gabriel is saddened by Zechariah's doubt when he is told that his elderly wife, Elizabeth, would bear a son. Because Zechariah didn't believe, the angel made him mute until the child, John, was born. Angels feel grief when we lack faith in God's word.

* * *

ANGELIC INSPIRATION

02

Types of Angels

Angels come in many forms and serve different purposes based on their rank and duties. Here are some types of angels:

Human Angels

These are angels who take on human form. They can walk among us, help us in times of need, and sometimes reveal themselves in mysterious ways. They are often undetectable, but their presence is felt through their actions.

Functions & Duties

Helping Humans in Need

Have you ever experienced someone appearing out of nowhere to help you, and then when you try to thank them, they're gone? It could have been an angel in human form, sent to help you at just the right time.

Present in Everyday Places

Angels in human form may be found anywhere—churches, hospitals, orphanages, or even as regular employees in unexpected places. They quietly carry out their mission of helping others, often without being noticed.

Saving Lives

Angels often save us from dangers we can't see. If a stranger advises you to avoid a particular road or warns you of potential harm, it could be an angelic intervention. Don't overlook such seemingly random acts of help—angels might be protecting you.

Dine with Angels

The Bible encourages us to welcome strangers because, as Hebrews 13:2 says, "many have entertained angels without knowing it." Angels might come to your home, share a meal, and leave you feeling uplifted. Just as Abraham unknowingly invited angels into his home in the Bible, we too might host angels in disguise.

Real-Life Encounter with an Angel

Ivy Olsen, a struggling single mother, experienced what she believes was an encounter with an angel in 1969. After her divorce, Ivy was having a particularly hard Thanksgiving with barely any food for her two boys. She only had three hotdogs, so she took her boys on a picnic to lift their spirits. After the picnic, her kids were still hungry, but Ivy had nothing else to give them.

When they returned to their apartment, they met an elderly woman who invited them to her home for a Thanksgiving dinner. The woman was warm and joyful, with a presence that felt almost electric. Ivy and her children enjoyed an abundant feast, and before leaving, the woman gave them gifts and enough leftovers to last them through the week.

The next day, Ivy went to thank the woman, but when she arrived at her apartment, it was empty. There was no furniture, no sign that anyone had lived there for weeks. The apartment manager confirmed that the unit had been vacant for 10-12 weeks. Ivy's encounter with this mysterious woman convinced her she had dined with an angel.

This story reminds us of the subtle, yet powerful, ways angels might touch our lives. Ivy's encounter, like many similar stories, leaves us with a sense of wonder and a belief that angels are watching over us, helping us when we least expect it.

This makes angels feel closer and more relatable—they aren't distant beings. They may be walking among us, intervening at critical moments, and leaving behind a sense of joy and comfort in their wake. Just as they helped Ivy in her time of need, angels are always working in our lives, even when we don't realize it.

Archangels

Archangels are among the highest-ranking angels, serving directly under God and carrying out major tasks on His behalf. Their name means "chief angel" or "angel of origin," signifying their leadership role.

Each of the three main archangels—Michael, Gabriel, and Raphael—has a specific role and unique powers, as their names suggest, and they often appear in critical moments in the Bible.

"Those who deliver messages of lesser importance are called angels; and those who proclaim messages of supreme importance are called archangels."

– Saint Gregory the Great

Michael ("Who is like God?")

Source: catholicdioceseofwichita

Michael is the warrior archangel, the protector of God's people and the leader of Heaven's armies. He's often depicted with a sword, ready to battle evil forces. Michael famously led the angels in the war against Lucifer and his rebellious followers, casting them out of Heaven. But his fight didn't stop there—now, Michael helps guard our souls against the temptations of evil and the lies that Satan tries to plant in our hearts. He's a spiritual warrior who defends us when we face struggles in life, especially in matters of faith.

In Revelation 12:7-8, Michael leads the charge in Heaven's battle:

"Now war arose in heaven, Michael and his angels fighting against the dragon. And the dragon and his angels fought back, but he was defeated, and there was no longer any place for them in heaven."

This powerful image shows that Michael not only fights for God but for all humanity, protecting us from the forces of darkness.

In Jude 1:9, Michael shows his humility and strength in a confrontation with the devil:

"But when the archangel Michael, contending with the devil, was disputing about the body of Moses, he did not presume to pronounce a blasphemous judgment, but said, 'The Lord rebuke you.'"

Even though Michael is powerful, he doesn't act on his own; he acknowledges that God alone is the ultimate judge.

St. Basil the Great, a Father of the Church,

"Michael, the Archangel, when challenged by the devil, did not bring against him an accusation of blasphemy, but simply said, 'The Lord rebuke you.'"

This quote reflects Archangel Michael's humility and reliance on God's authority, even in his role as a powerful defender of Heaven.

Gabriel ("God's Power")

Gabriel is the messenger archangel, often sent by God to deliver important news. One of his most famous moments is when he appears to the Virgin Mary to announce the birth of Jesus, saying:

"You will conceive and give birth to a son, and you are to call him Jesus." (Luke 1:31)

Gabriel's role in the Bible is often tied to delivering life-changing messages. He was sent to tell Zechariah that his wife Elizabeth would give birth to John the Baptist, even though they were both too old by human standards. Gabriel was also the angel who explained visions to the prophet Daniel and was there to comfort and guide people in their times of confusion.

In everyday life, Gabriel is like the voice of reason—the one who shows up when you need clarity or direction. His name alone reminds us that God's power is always at work, even when we feel lost.

Raphael ("God Heals")

Raphael, whose name means "God heals," is the archangel associated with healing and guidance. His story is told in the Book of Tobit in the Old Testament, where he helps Tobit and his son, Tobias, through physical and spiritual healing. Raphael is often seen as a divine guide for those who are sick or lost.

In life, Raphael represents the unseen help we receive when we need healing—whether it's emotional, physical, or spiritual. When you're going through tough times and suddenly find comfort or a solution you hadn't expected, it might just be Raphael working behind the scenes to guide you back to health and peace.

Paramahansa Yogananda:

"Archangels are exalted beings whose thought of God is uninterrupted, who embody divine will and the manifestation of divine love."

This speaks to the high spiritual status and purpose of Archangels as intermediaries between God and humans, representing divine power, protection, and guidance.

03

Behind the Scenes: The Workings of Angels

Archangels are not just ancient beings from Biblical times. Their presence is felt even today. Michael stands with us when we feel overwhelmed by life's battles, Gabriel brings clarity when we're confused or struggling with big decisions, and Raphael guides us toward healing when we're broken or in pain. They are like divine helpers who show up in our lives at just the right moment, protecting us, guiding us, and healing us in ways we might not always see but can definitely feel.

Just as the Bible promises in

1 Thessalonians 4:16:

"For the Lord himself will descend from heaven with a cry of command, with the voice of an archangel, and with the sound of the trumpet of God."

These powerful angels will one day return with Christ to complete their work, but until then, they are still here—watching over us, guiding us, and defending us.

Archangels can feel distant or otherworldly, but they are often more involved in our lives than we realize. Think of the times when you've found unexpected strength in a crisis or received clarity when making a difficult decision—these might be moments where archangels like Michael, Gabriel, or Raphael were guiding you. Even today, they continue to fulfil their divine duties, helping us as we navigate life's challenges.

While many people are familiar with the well-known Archangels Michael, Gabriel, and Raphael, there are four other powerful Archangels whose roles are equally significant, though they are less commonly mentioned in modern texts. These Archangels, once revered in early Christian traditions, are featured prominently in the Book of Enoch, a text removed from the canon centuries ago. Here's a closer look at these intriguing figures:

1. Uriel: Meaning "Fire of God,"

Source: shutterstock

Uriel is known as the Archangel of Repentance and the Damned. He was assigned as a Watcher over Hades, guiding souls through their final judgments. Uriel is also recognized as the patron of the Sacrament of Confirmation, symbolizing purification and enlightenment.

2. Raguel:

Translating to "Friend of God," Raguel is the Archangel of Justice and Fairness. Known also as Sealtiel, he serves as the guardian of righteous order and is associated with the Sacrament of Holy Orders, reflecting his role in guiding spiritual leaders.

3. Zerachiel:

Often called Saraqael, Baruchel, or Sariel, Zerachiel means "God's command." He is the Archangel of God's Judgment and the patron of the Sacrament of Matrimony. His role involves overseeing divine justice and the sanctity of marriage.

4. Remiel:

Known by names like Jerahmeel, Jehudial, or Jeremiel, Remiel means "Thunder of God," "Mercy of God," or "Compassion of God." As the Archangel of Hope and Faith, Remiel is also associated with dreams and the Sacrament of Anointing of the Sick, providing comfort and healing.

These Archangels represent critical aspects of divine intervention and guidance, offering insight into the roles and functions of celestial beings in spiritual traditions.

Cherubim: The True Guardians of the Divine

When we think of Cherubim, many picture cute, chubby baby angels with tiny wings. But that's far from the biblical reality!

What Are Cherubim?

Cherubim, or Cherubs in the plural form, are powerful, symbolic figures mentioned in the Bible. They first appear in the Book of Genesis, where they are assigned to guard the Garden of Eden with flaming swords after Adam and Eve's expulsion (Genesis 3:24).

Not Your Typical Angels

The Bible describes Cherubim very differently from the cute images we often see. According to the prophet Ezekiel,

Cherubim

Source: shutterstock

Cherubim are majestic and awe-inspiring beings. They have four faces—those of a human, a lion, an ox, and an eagle—and four wings. This strange, powerful appearance reflects their role as protectors of divine spaces. The image of angels with eyes covering their bodies comes from biblical and religious texts, particularly in descriptions of certain types of angels, like the Seraphim and Cherubim, found in the Old Testament of the Bible. For instance, in the Book of Ezekiel (Chapter 10), there is a vision of angels, specifically Cherubim, with eyes on their wings and bodies. These eyes symbolize their ability to perceive and be aware of everything happening in the universe.

In a more relatable sense, having eyes all over could be compared to having a heightened sense of awareness, knowledge, or insight—similar to how surveillance cameras cover all angles of a space. Another example could be in nature: creatures like spiders or certain insects that have multiple eyes allow them to see threats or prey from many directions at once.

Symbolically, it's like saying someone has "eyes in the back of their head"—a phrase often used to describe someone who seems to always be aware of what's going on around them. It could represent vigilance, wisdom, or being all-knowing in various aspects of life.

Roles and Responsibilities

Cherubim are not just decorative figures. They play crucial roles in the Bible:

1. Guardians of Sacred Spaces:

They guard important divine realms, like the Garden of Eden.

2. Keepers of the Ark:

In the construction of the Ark of the Covenant, Cherubim were carved to stand over the ark, symbolizing their role in protecting God's presence.

3. Throne Angels:

In visions like Ezekiel's, Cherubim are seen around God's throne, symbolizing their role in guarding His holiness and majesty.

Jewish Folklore

In Jewish tradition, Cherubim are sometimes referred to as "Merkabah" or "Throne Angels," reflecting their role in protecting and surrounding the divine presence.

Why It Matters

Understanding Cherubim's true nature helps us appreciate their role in spiritual traditions. They are not merely cute figures but are essential in safeguarding divine realms and ensuring the sanctity of God's presence.

Seraphim: The Fiery Angels

What Are Seraphim?

The term "Seraphim" comes from a Hebrew word meaning "burning ones." These angels are often associated with intense purity and love. They are only fully described in the Book of Isaiah, where the prophet Isaiah has a vision of them in heaven.

Distinct Features:

- Wings: Seraphim have six wings. They use two for flying, while the other four cover their face and feet. This is because they are so close to God's overwhelming glory that they need to shield themselves from its brightness.

- Role: They are positioned above God's throne and are known for their continuous praise of God. Their eternal hymn, "Holy, holy, holy is the LORD Almighty," is a central prayer in both Jewish and Christian traditions, emphasizing God's supreme holiness.

Artistic Depictions:

In art, Seraphim are often shown as red, symbolizing their fiery nature. They might also be depicted with a flaming sword inscribed with "holy, holy, holy."

Key Difference from Cherubim:

- Cherubim: Have four faces (ox, lion, man, and eagle) and four wings. They guard sacred spaces and are depicted in books like Genesis and Ezekiel.

- Seraphim: Have six wings and are primarily described in Isaiah. They are associated with direct praise of God and are sometimes seen as the highest rank of angels due to their proximity to God.

Symbolism:

The Seraphim's role and appearance highlight their deep devotion and purity.

The imagery of fire and burning emphasizes their role in cleansing and sanctifying.

The Four Living Creatures: Heavenly Wonders Unveiled

What Are They?

In the Bible's Book of Revelation, we encounter the Four Living Creatures—mysterious and powerful beings that blend elements of both the Seraphim and Cherubim.

Stunning Features:

- Wings & Vision: They boast six wings like the Seraphim and are covered in eyes, symbolizing their all-seeing nature.

- Distinct Faces: Each creature has four distinct faces—lion, ox, man and eagle—reflecting the might and majesty of the Cherubim.

Purpose & Worship:

- Divine Reverence: Their primary role is to continuously praise and worship the Lamb, Jesus Christ, offering the same profound reverence they once gave to God the Father. This act of worship signifies their ultimate dedication and divine status.

Mystical Insight:

- Prophetic Connections: These beings are pivotal in prophetic ministry, offering deep insights into both past events and future revelations. Their role emphasizes the extraordinary connection between the heavenly realm and earthly understanding.

Why They Matter:

The Four Living Creatures are not only awe-inspiring but also essential in bridging the divine and human realms. Their complex forms and roles highlight the profound mystery and majesty of God's creation.

Quote by Charles Spurgeon on Seraphim and Cherubim:

"Amid the splendors of heaven stand the seraphim and cherubim, blazing with love and flying with wings of burning zeal, who are never weary of crying out, 'Holy, holy, holy is the Lord God Almighty.'"

This captures the reverence, passion, and devotion of both Seraphim and Cherubim in their ceaseless worship of God's holiness and majesty.

Guardian Angels: Our Divine Companions

What Are Guardian Angels?

Guardian Angels are believed to be divine protectors assigned to each person from birth until death. Their role is to guide, protect, and support us throughout our lives. This concept isn't unique to Christianity—it appears in other religions and philosophies too.

Key Insights About Guardian Angels:

1. Always Present: Your Guardian Angel is with you from the moment you're born until your last breath, providing unwavering protection and guidance.

2. Eternal Existence: Guardian Angels aren't created at birth. They were among the thousands of angels created by God at the beginning of time.

3. Unique Roles: Not all angels are Guardian Angels. There's a hierarchy, and only certain angels are chosen for this sacred role.

4. One for One: Each person has one Guardian Angel assigned exclusively to them. This angel is a constant, dedicated presence in your life.

5. Guidance, Not Coercion: While your Guardian Angel can't force you to make good choices, they offer advice and suggestions to help you follow the right path toward Heaven.

6. Everlasting Support: They never leave your side, both in this life and the next, ensuring you're never alone.

7. Not a Departed Loved One: Guardian Angels are unique spiritual beings created by God, not spirits of deceased loved ones.

8. Nameless: Guardian Angels don't have personal names. While some angels like Michael and Gabriel are named in the Scriptures, your Guardian Angel's name is not for us to determine.

9. Warriors of Light: Far from being delicate, your Guardian Angel is a strong, courageous protector who fights for you in life's battles.

10. Messengers of God: They relay messages between you and God, ensuring you receive divine guidance and understanding.

Why It Matters:

Understanding the role and nature of your Guardian Angel helps you appreciate the constant divine support in your life. These celestial beings are not just protectors but also companions on your spiritual journey, ensuring you are guided, protected, and loved every step of the way.

Perhaps guardian angels are not the shields we imagine them to be, but rather silent companions on the path of our own becoming. When tragedy strikes, and we call for rescue, their silence may not be indifference, but a reflection of something deeper—an invitation to rise beyond our fear, to discover our strength in the heart of the storm.

What if the role of a guardian angel is not to prevent every wound, but to help us transform it? Like a light that doesn't banish the darkness but helps us find our way within it, they guide us—

not away from pain, but through it, allowing us to emerge wiser, stronger, and more attuned to the mystery of life.

Could it be that the greatest protection they offer is not from external harm, but from the fear that we are alone in our suffering? Perhaps they save us not by preventing tragedy, but by teaching us that even in our deepest despair, we are capable of healing, of hope, of becoming something more than we were before.

In this way, they don't save us from the darkness—they help us become the light within it.

04

Three Divine Powers Bestowed by Angels

Unlocking Angelic Powers

How Angels Empower Us. When you align yourself with God's word and embrace the Holy Spirit, angels can bestow powerful blessings

upon you. These divine messengers bring three distinct gifts when you live a holy and righteous life.

1. Enhanced Discernment

Angels with Gods approval can grant you the gift of discernment, allowing you to perceive the true intentions of others and understand situations with clarity. Just as Jesus knew the thoughts of the Pharisees, you too can develop the ability to sense underlying truths and protect yourself from deceit and misfortune. This spiritual insight helps you make wise decisions and navigate life with greater awareness.

2. Joy and Peace

The presence of angels often fills you with an unshakable sense of joy and peace.

This divine joy goes beyond worldly pleasures, providing a deep, lasting contentment. It also instills confidence, as reflected in the Biblical verse, "The righteous are as bold as a lion." While not giving you superhuman abilities, this gift enhances your spiritual strength and assurance, empowering you to speak and act with confidence.

3. Healing of Physical and Spiritual Ailments

Angels can facilitate healing, both physically and spiritually, by channeling God's grace. Whether dealing with ailments like depression, anxiety, or physical pain, angels play a role in the healing process, as demonstrated by the angel stirring the waters of Bethesda. Faith and alignment with Christ's will are essential for this healing to manifest, reflecting the ongoing divine care and support in your life.

Living a Holy Life

To fully experience these angelic gifts, it's crucial to maintain a holy life. This means living in accordance with God's teachings and nurturing your spiritual connection. While these three gifts are significant, angels may offer even more blessings as you deepen your spiritual journey.

Embrace these divine powers and live in a way that honors the presence of angels in your life.

05

How to Invite and Activate Angelic Presence in Your Life

Angels can have a profound impact on your life, but activating their presence requires intentional spiritual practices. Here's how you can invite these divine helpers into your life

1. Pray Without Ceasing

Continuous prayer is key. When you earnestly pray for spiritual insight and a deeper connection with the divine, God listens. As the Bible says, if even flawed humans know how to give good gifts, how much more will God bless those who seek Him earnestly?

Amos 3:7 reminds us that God reveals His plans to His servants. By praying regularly, you open yourself to spiritual revelations and angelic guidance.

2. Believe Over Doubt

Faith is crucial. Jesus said that even faith as small as a mustard seed can move mountains. Trust in God and His plans, and acknowledge that angels are real helpers, not beings to be worshiped above God. Your faith strengthens your connection with the divine and allows you to experience angelic support more fully.

3. Live a Life of Consecration and Holiness

Holiness attracts holiness. To engage with angels who are pure and aligned with God, strive to live a life that pleases Him. Avoid the pitfalls of sin and seek forgiveness through Christ. Your commitment to holiness sets a foundation for divine interactions and spiritual growth.

4. Empower Angels with God's Word

The Bible is a powerful tool. Regularly reading and proclaiming Scripture not only strengthens your bond with God but also empowers angels to work effectively in your life. Make Bible study and prayer a daily practice to witness the mighty power of God and His angels.

5. Align Your Motives with God's Kingdom

Angels work to further God's kingdom, not personal agendas. Ensure your intentions are aligned with God's will and embody agape love—selfless, unconditional love. Your motives should reflect a commitment to God's purpose, enhancing the effectiveness of angelic assistance in your life.

By integrating these practices into your daily routine, you open the door to angelic guidance and support, enriching your spiritual journey and deepening your connection with God.

06 Signs to Detect Angelic Presence Around You

Angels often communicate through subtle signs. Here's how to recognize their presence:

1. Goosebumps

Have you ever experienced sudden goosebumps or an inexplicable shiver?

This physical reaction can be a sign that angels are nearby, especially if it happens during a significant moment or decision. These chills can also be a reassuring nudge that you're on the right path, like during a job interview or a crucial life choice.

2. Unexpected Scents

A sudden, pleasant aroma—something you've never smelled before—could be an angelic sign. This fragrance, often accompanied by a sense of peace and comfort, might indicate that an angel is present, offering you reassurance and guidance.

3. Illuminating Dreams

Angels often communicate through dreams when your mind is most open. Watch for recurring themes or vivid imagery that stands out. Keeping a dream journal can help you decode these messages. These dreams might also serve as warnings or reminders of what's important in your life.

4. Flashes of Light

Have you noticed flashes or shimmering lights, often out of the corner of your eye? These can be signs of angelic activity. The color of the light might offer clues: orange for optimism, green for increased power, and blue or purple for relaxation and calm.

5. Deep Sense of Calm

A strong feeling that you're not alone, especially during stressful times, can indicate an angel's presence. This sense of support and companionship might be particularly comforting when you're feeling isolated or misunderstood. It's a reminder that you're never truly alone.

6. Unexpected Success and Favors

Angel encounters often come with unexpected blessings. If you find yourself receiving sudden favors or opportunities, it could be a sign that angelic help is at work in your life. These unexpected boosts can signal that you're being guided and supported from a higher realm.

Stay attuned to these signs, and remember that angels are often working behind the scenes to guide and support you on your journey.

Surrounded by angels, I find peace in the unseen, knowing their silent wings carry eternal love and protection

Where Were the Angels During Christ's Crucifixion?

While the Bible does not explicitly state that angels were present at the crucifixion of Jesus, their roles around this pivotal event suggest their significant involvement in the divine drama of His death and resurrection.

Garden of Gethsemane

Source: istockphoto

1. In the Garden of Gethsemane:

Before His arrest, Jesus withdrew to the Garden of Gethsemane to pray. In this agonizing moment, as He faced the weight of His impending sacrifice, an angel appeared to Him to strengthen Him. This event is recorded in Luke 22:43, highlighting the angel's role in providing spiritual fortitude to Jesus during His most vulnerable time.

During the Crucifixion

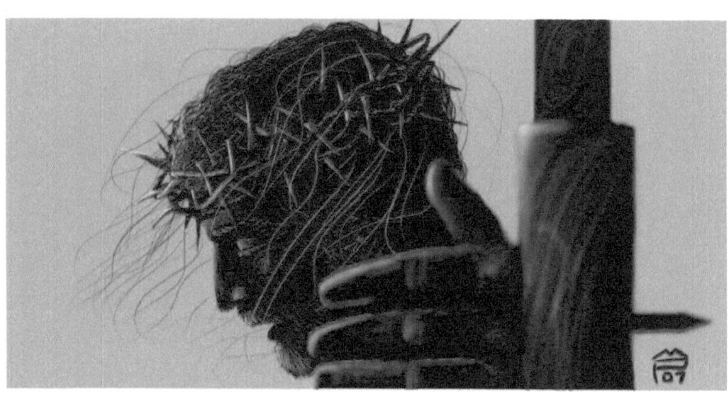

2. During the Crucifixion:

Although the Gospels do not directly mention angels at the crucifixion, theological interpretations often suggest their presence in a more observational capacity. In Matthew 26:53, Jesus speaks of His ability to call upon legions of angels if He wished, indicating that they were available to Him but He chose to proceed with His sacrificial mission without their intervention. This absence of direct angelic intervention underscores Jesus' voluntary acceptance of His suffering.

At The Resurrection

Source: reedimggod

3. At the Resurrection:

Angels play a prominent role immediately following the crucifixion. When Jesus' body lay in the tomb, angels were actively involved in the resurrection event. They rolled away the stone from the entrance of the tomb and announced Jesus' resurrection to the women who came to anoint His body. This is detailed in several Gospel accounts: Matthew 28:2-6, Mark 16:5-7, Luke 24:4-7, and John 20:12. Their presence not only marked the divine triumph over death but also provided the first witnesses to the miraculous event.

While the Bible does not describe angels actively participating in the crucifixion itself, their involvement in the events surrounding it—from providing strength in Gethsemane to heralding the resurrection—emphasizes their crucial role in the divine plan of salvation.

Here's a quote from the Gospel of Matthew about angels during the resurrection of Christ:

"His appearance was like lightning, and his clothing white as snow. The guards were so afraid of him that they shook and became like dead men." — Matthew 28:3-4

This describes the angel who rolled away the stone from Jesus' tomb, symbolizing divine power and the profound role of angels in key moments of Christian faith, such as the resurrection.

08

Real-Life Encounters with Angelic Beings: Stories that Inspire Awe

There are numerous stories shared by people who claim to have had real-life encounters with angels, often during critical moments of their lives, where these experiences deeply moved them or even changed their life course. Here's a fictional retelling of such an encounter with a dramatic and emotional ending

* * *

The Silent Guardian

Sarah had always been a skeptic, a woman grounded in reality, always dismissing the supernatural as just stories or coincidences. But her life was about to change in ways she could never have imagined.

One rainy evening, as Sarah drove down a winding mountain road, the tires of her car lost traction. In an instant, her car veered off the road and plummeted down a steep ravine. Panic seized her heart as the car flipped and crashed into a tree. The world around her became a blur of pain, shattered glass, and the sound of metal twisting.

Her body was pinned, her breathing shallow, and darkness slowly crept into her vision. It felt like the end.

Suddenly, amidst the chaos, a light, warm and steady, filled the space inside the mangled car.

A figure, cloaked in an ethereal glow, appeared beside her, its presence calming the storm of fear and pain in her heart. She couldn't see its face clearly, but its form radiated peace, strength, and a love that was beyond words.

The being touched her arm lightly, and Sarah felt a wave of warmth rush through her body, numbing the pain and easing her breathing. It whispered gently, though its lips never moved. "You're not alone. Help is on the way."

In that moment, Sarah felt a surge of strength she hadn't known she possessed. She was able to lift her head, her panic gone, her focus returning. Just as she was about to ask who this being was, the distant wail of sirens filled the air. The figure smiled softly and disappeared, leaving her in the stillness of the wreckage, but she wasn't afraid anymore.

Rescue workers soon arrived and pulled her from the car. Though badly injured, she was alive, and she clung to the memory of the being who had saved her in those critical moments.

Weeks passed as Sarah healed in the hospital. But the encounter with the angel stayed with her, burning brightly in her thoughts. Her life, once dominated by doubt, began to shift in profound ways.

One night, as she lay in bed recovering, she had a vivid dream. She saw the same glowing figure standing at the foot of her bed. This time, she saw it more clearly—a beautiful, radiant angel with golden wings and a kind smile. Tears filled her eyes as she asked, "Why me? Why did you save me?"

The angel looked at her with deep compassion. "Your journey isn't over, Sarah. There's more for you to do. The world still needs your light. Never doubt that you are loved."

Sarah woke up in tears, overwhelmed with gratitude and the realization that her life had meaning and purpose beyond what she had ever known. The angel had touched her soul in a way that would drive her to live with more love, compassion, and faith than she ever thought possible.

From that day forward, Sarah dedicated her life to helping others—sharing her story, offering comfort to those in need, and becoming a source of strength for those who felt lost.

* * *

This type of story resonates because it speaks to the universal human longing for connection, meaning, and the belief that we are not alone in our darkest moments. Whether one believes in angels or not, these encounters often serve as powerful symbols of hope and the strength that emerges from within.

Biblical Encounters:

1. Abraham and the Three Visitors (Genesis 18):

Abraham was visited by three men, one of whom is considered a divine messenger or a manifestation of God. They delivered the miraculous news that his wife, Sarah, would bear a son despite her old age. This encounter is a profound moment in the biblical narrative, showcasing divine intervention and promise.

Quote by Billy Graham on biblical encounters with angels:

"Angels have a much more important place in the Bible than the devil and his demons. Angels are mentioned hundreds of times. They are God's messengers, dispatched to do His bidding and to intervene in the affairs of men."

This highlights the frequent and significant role angels play throughout Scripture, serving as messengers, protectors, and agents of God's will.

Jacob's ladder

Source: quantumtorah

2. Jacob's Ladder (Genesis 28:10-17):

In a dream, Jacob saw a ladder reaching from earth to heaven with angels ascending and descending upon it. This vision was not only a powerful symbol of the connection between heaven and earth but also reaffirmed God's covenant with Jacob, marking him as a key figure in the divine plan.

3. Angel of the Lord and Gideon (Judges 6:11-24):

Gideon encountered an angel who delivered a call to lead Israel against the Midianites. To confirm the message, the angel performed a miraculous sign, demonstrating divine approval and empowering Gideon for his pivotal role in Israel's history.

Gabriel meeting Mary

Source: christianity.com

4. Angel Gabriel and Mary (Luke 1:26-38):

The Angel Gabriel appeared to Mary, announcing that she would conceive and bear Jesus, the Son of God. This encounter is one of the most significant in Christian tradition, marking the beginning of the fulfillment of divine promises through the birth of Christ.

5. Angels at Jesus' Resurrection (Matthew 28:1-7; Mark 16:5-7; Luke 24:4-7; John 20:12):

Following Jesus' crucifixion, angels were present at His tomb, announcing His resurrection to Mary Magdalene and other women. Their role in this momentous event underscores their significance in the divine narrative of redemption and hope.

Personal Experience:

Date: March 17, 2021

My journey into understanding angelic beings took a profound turn when I had a personal encounter. One night, as I was sleeping, I dreamt of a towering figure of Michael, the Warrior Angel. His presence was overwhelming, bathed in brilliant light that made it difficult to see his face. However, the light had a distinct bluish-purple hue, which seemed to envelop his massive wings. The next day, my research revealed that this color is indeed associated with Michael, adding a layer of depth and significance to my experience.

This encounter filled me with awe and led me to delve deeper into understanding these divine beings and their roles in our lives. It became clear to me that angelic beings are not just distant figures but active participants in our spiritual journey.

Conclusion:

As you read this book, I hope you will gain insight into the presence and power of angels in your own life. Look for the divine in everyday moments and remain open to the guidance and support they offer.

Always remember:

"In the quiet moments when doubt casts a shadow, remember the unseen wings that have always guided your path, and may you walk forward with faith, knowing you are never alone."

www.ingramcontent.com/pod-product-compliance
Lightning Source LLC
LaVergne TN
LVHW091121150826
845673LV00002B/926